WORSHIP COME TO ITS SENSES

WORSHIP COME TO ITS SENSES

Don E. Saliers

ABINGDON PRESS
NASHVILLE

WORSHIP COME TO ITS SENSES

Copyright © 1996 by Abingdon Press

This book is printed on recycled, acid-free paper.

Library of Congress Cataloging-in-Publication Data

Saliers, Don E., 1937–
  Worship come to its senses / Don E. Saliers.
      p.   cm.
  Includes bibliographical references.
  ISBN 0-687-01458-1 (alk. paper)
    1. Public worship.   I. Title.
  BV15.S26   1996
  264—dc20   95-44697
                                                                          CIP

Scripture quotations, unless otherwise noted, are from the New Revised Standard Version Bible, copyright © 1989 by the Division of Christian Education of the National Council of the Churches of Christ in the United States of America.

Those noted NIV are taken from the Holy Bible: New International Version. Copyright © 1973, 1978, 1984 by the International Bible Society. Used by permission of Zondervan Bible Publishers.

Grateful acknowledgment is made to Hope Publishing Company for permission to use excerpts from the following:
  "I Come With Joy," by Brian Wren (p. 19), © 1971;
  "For Musicians," by Eric Routley (p. 34), © 1977;
  "Lord of the Dance" (in its entirety), by Sydney Carter (pp. 45-46), © 1963;
  "God Give Us Freedom to Lament," by Brian Wren (p. 58), © 1993;
  "When Pain and Terror Strike by Chance," by Brian Wren (p. 58), © 1993;
  "Hope of the World," by Georgia Harkness (p. 66), © 1954;
  "When in Our Music God Is Glorified," by Fred Pratt Green (p. 89), © 1971.

"God of the Sparrow God of the Whale," by Jaroslav Vajda (p. 31), © 1983, is used by permission of the author.

"Lift Every Voice and Sing," by James Weldon Johnson (p. 84), © 1921, renewed, is used by permission of Edward B. Marks Music Company.

96 97 98 99 00 01 02 03 04 05 — 10 9 8 7 6 5 4 3 2 1

MANUFACTURED IN THE UNITED STATES OF AMERICA

To
Hoyt L. Hickman,
pastoral-liturgical shepherd,
mentoring colleague,
cherished friend;
and to
Martha Whitmore Hickman,
gifted writer,
companion soul

CONTENTS

Acknowledgments

Most books are communal acts. Conversations arouse and help shape images and ideas. Insights come from unexpected places. Friends and colleagues encourage and challenge the emerging pages. This little book is no exception, arising as it does from years of workshops, retreats, and worship in local congregations across the country. I am grateful to many who think of themselves as ordinary Christians who listened and responded.

I am especially indebted to students and colleagues at Candler School of Theology who patiently listened me into clarity on the themes in this book. Students in my worship course and in the seminar in liturgical theology were wonderful midwives to some of the material here, when it was still in primitive form. Lectures at St. John's University, Collegeville, Minnesota, and the Heinsohn Lectureship at University United Methodist Church in Austin, Texas, allowed me to sound publicly these themes. Special thanks go

Aknowledgments

to Ron Anderson for his sharp-eyed, insightful reading of the manuscript in its later stages.

But this book would not be what it is without the encouragement and editorial grace of Ulrike Guthrie of Abingdon Press. To her and all the others, my heart-felt gratitude.

INTRODUCTION

If someone says to us "Come to your senses!" that often means "Wake up and smell the coffee!" We are either unaware, or distracted, or deliberately ignoring what we see. Something is hidden from us in a relationship or in a course of action. Our behavior may be doing injury and we are unaware of it. Sometimes our attitudes and personal feelings may even be destructive, either of ourselves or of others, and we ignore them. So a good friend may actually do us an act of kindness by admonishing us, "Come to your senses about this."

We not only have occasion to say this to one another as friends or as family, there are also times when we must say this to whole groups of people. Institutions—whether schools, businesses, churches, or governments—need such a reminder as well. Indeed, haven't we in the Christian community cried out to a whole society, "Let's come to our senses about nuclear proliferation, about abuse, hunger, and violence, about corruption and injustice"? So citizens may actually do our common culture an act of kindness by admonishing us, "Wake up! The time has come to think, feel, and act differently." The American Civil Rights movement was such a collective coming to our senses.

The Costs and Consequences of Coming to Our Senses

Coming to our senses may have modest or grave consequences, depending upon the seriousness of the problem. To come to terms with our having overextended our schedule is one thing, to come to terms with an ambiguous flirtation another, and to come to terms with a destructive addiction yet another matter. And, as we all know too well, to come to our collective senses about abuse, violence, or corruption is enormously demanding and complex. All too often it takes a deep crisis, such as the April 1995 bombing in Oklahoma City, to get our attention focused. Even then we may not come to terms with the deeper implications of the crisis once it has passed from our TV screens as a media event. "Out of sight, out of mind" is increasingly true of our moral and religious practices.

Coming to our senses requires both the deepening of thought and the awakening of conscience. It requires deeper feeling and sustained discernment of our actual practices and attitudes. Stepping outside our routine behavior and our habitual attitudes and practices is not easy. To see ourselves from another point of view, and to discern what keeps us from flourishing, requires questions from the "outside." Gaining critical distance from what lies so close to our ways of thinking, feeling, and acting often comes at some cost. Clearly, coming to our senses asks us to think and feel and intend life in a new and fresh way. This is especially true of our moral and religious practices.

When in these pages we ask about Christian worship, the selfsame matters are at stake. As one who cares for the gospel and for the living witness and quality of the way we worship God, I find myself asking about what we habitually do when we gather. I wonder where such qualities as awe and wonderment, truthfulness and authenticity, and delight and hope are found. I ask myself why these qualities are so often missing or diminished in our worshiping assemblies. The current debates about "traditional" and "contemporary" worship seem to raise such questions at every turn. So this book is an invitation to think again about how and why we worship God, and to awaken our hearts and minds to a fresh perspective.

A Basic Question

The chapters that follow arise from a restlessness with worship "as we've always done it" in many of our congregations. In speaking with people in several ecumenically diverse traditions, but especially in "mainline" (or "old line") Protestant traditions, I detect among many—laity and clergy alike—the same restlessness. After the past quarter-century's widespread effort at liturgical reform there is a deeper hunger for a renewed connection between liturgy and life, between common prayer and ministry. So we must *true* ask again in our time the basic double question: *What for makes Christian worship true and relevant, and how uu* *cos worship can our liturgical gatherings shape and express authentic Christian faith and life in the world of everyday?*

There is no one right way to approach these issues. Yet there are certain marks of such worship. In this book I will refer to these as essential qualities. The "senses" of worship that name these qualities, which make up the four chapters here, are not intended to be exhaustive. Yet tracing these will address some of the issues confronting all who seek to plan, lead, and participate in worship "in spirit and in truth."

The Senses of Awe, Delight, Truthfulness, and Hope

The four essential qualities that characterize true and relevant Christian worship and that call for renewed attention are awe, delight, truthfulness, and hope. These are called "senses" because they name patterns in human experience of God. These are also themes in praying, singing, and proclaiming good news in our gathering about the book, the font of baptism, and the Lord's table. By asking how these four qualities are sensed, or why they may be absent or diminished, I hope to shed light on what may be done to restore or to deepen them in our worshiping congregations.

Along the way we will also attend to the manner in which the physical senses are crucial to the recovery of awe, delight, truthfulness, and hope. For worship depends upon our capabilities of sensing presence, of hearing, seeing, touching, moving, smelling, and tasting. This is perhaps especially so when one or more of those senses is limited, as in specific disability, simply because Christian worship is physically, socially, and culturally embodied. Prayer and song constitute the language of the human heart. And knowledge of God is never purely intellectual. The words we speak and hear (or see in the case of signing) depend radically upon the nonverbal languages of Christian liturgical action. Such nonverbal languages involve the physical senses. We must deal, then, with the relations between physical senses, feelings, more complex emotions, and the *sense* of God. It is still true that spiritual knowledge of God comes through the physical senses in the Spirit-gifted social body we call the church.

Yearning for More, Not Settling for Less

How may we find again, for our present circumstances, the sense of awe and mystery, the sense of delight and spontaneity, the sense of knowing and being known by God truthfully, and the sense of hope in a confusing and violent world? When we sing "The hopes and fears of all the years are met in thee tonight," what hopes and fears do we bring? When, in Advent, we sing, "O come, O come, Emmanuel," what longings for our world and for our lives are made present? If we sing "Spirit of the living God, fall afresh on me," what do we expect? These questions point in the direction of a different kind of preparation, and a more attentive participation. Why do we settle for so little when God offers so much in Word, sacrament, and song?

I vividly recall a worship convocation in Buckhannon, West Virginia, in the summer of 1975. It was the first time United Methodists had used what was then the new service of baptismal renewal for the whole congregation. The singing was strong, the prayers fresh, and the preaching a powerful claiming of living out our baptismal life in Christ. The act of renewal following the prayer over the water took us beyond what we had experienced before: "Remember your baptism, and be thankful!" echoed again and again throughout the sanctuary. Following the service, several persons came to the sacristy to testify to their experience. I will never forget what one person asked, knowing what she had encountered, "Did we celebrate a sacrament here or hold a revival? I couldn't tell the difference!" That was liturgy come to our senses, in all the senses of the term.

Later, in thinking over what had occurred in that worship service, some of us noted that we could recall in great detail much of what we read, preached, and prayed because of the hospitality and the reverence of the whole service. It seemed like a day of low humidity (even though it was not), clear air, and sunlight. The details of the liturgy were *cared for,* and *cared about.* Several people observed that all who led—from musicians to readers, from dancers to the presiding ministers—were "present and alive." The secret was in the way in which the open, welcoming style of *all* who led made the congregation's participation vital, even though some of the texts and ritual actions were new. In and through the physical senses, and all who were involved, a sense of presence was given and received. Despite all our differences, we felt both at home and strangely expectant, open to something beyond *our* doing. In and through our seeing, hearing, touching, and moving, the sense of God's grace meeting us came alive. We knew our baptism was real because we were being known by the One into whom we had been baptized, whether early or later in life.

Like that assembly for worship twenty years ago, many people today are yearning for a truly evangelical and sacramental liturgy. In the chapters that follow, I will trace what might be called a double journey—a journey toward the mystery of God as well as into the depths of our humanity in God's presence. The first chapter explores the sense of awe: why it is essential to Christian worship, why it seems so missing, and how we may begin its recovery. The second explores the sense of delight: its central role in the worship of God, why it is so rare, and how it may be restored. The third raises the question of truth and integrity: why these are essential and so difficult to establish, and what may be done to render worship as true prayer. The fourth and final chapter explores why hope is native to authentic Christian worship, and what affections and dispositions we need to cultivate in order to celebrate the gospel of God's promise and to live in that hope.

CHAPTER ONE

The Sense of Awe

◆

I come with joy to meet my Lord,
forgiven, loved and free,
in awe and wonder to recall
his life laid down for me.
—BRIAN WREN, "I COME WITH JOY"

Recently, following a Sunday service in a Protestant church of some nine hundred members, I overheard a worshiper say to her companion, "Whatever happened to awe?" That question prompted me to think back over what had taken place in the previous hour. There had certainly been a sense of friendly welcome, and the informal singing of favorite hymns and songs had reminded me of my own childhood experience of the Sunday school assembly. The children's "moment" had been lively, focusing on how taking care of our pets can symbolize God's love. The choir had sung a rousing arrangement of "Standing on the Promises," and the sermon had been punctuated with helpful insights on dealing with stress.

She was right. There had been no suggestion of awe or wonder. Was she right to expect this? Did she have in mind some earlier time or perhaps another style of worship? Were she and her friend simply being snobbish? I don't think so. These are questions which occur to many of us about our responses to much current worship in our churches.

It is, of course, all too easy to associate awe and mystery with highly liturgical traditions, such as Eastern Orthodoxy, Roman Catholicism before the Second Vatican Council, or High Church Anglicanism. But I suspect this is not what she had in mind. The plain fact is that much of our worship in contemporary American churches, Protestant and Roman Catholic alike, is domesticated. It is pleasant, even user-friendly, but something is missing at the heart of our practices as well as our theology: awe in the presence of God.

Perhaps the very word "awe" is no longer used by many to refer to worship at all. When a twelve-year-old exclaims that a new video game or a sports figure is "awesome," it becomes harder to make the connection with the experience of worship. Lying behind the devaluation of the word is a complex shift in cultural patterns of perception. When our senses are continually bombarded with intensified visual or sound stimulation in entertainment and mass media, it is natural that our way of naming experiences will be changed. Changes in our use of the term "awe" signal changes in what we find interesting and what engages our attention. Is there something deeper here than shifts in popular culture? Or should we simply concede that contemporary Americans of certain age groups are no longer capable of experiencing awe of God?

It would be foolish and unfair to say that we can no longer experience awe or wonder, though many people are not familiar with these concepts as they are expressed in biblical language and images. The question is, How do we make the connection between awe and worship without the language and the images? This requires awakening to the reality to which the language refers. There is still the sense of awe named in the Scriptures, especially in the psalms, and in familiar hymns. The widely beloved hymn, "How Great Thou Art," echoes the psalms and prophets when it sings, "When I in awesome wonder consider all the worlds thy hands have made." Psalm 8 resounds with this sense of beholding the creation. And Psalm 89 declares:

Let the heavens praise your wonders, O LORD,
your faithfulness in the assembly of the holy ones.
. . . .
who is as mighty as you, O LORD?
Your faithfulness surrounds you. (Psalm 89:5, 8)

Awakening to Awe in Nature

A childhood memory keeps coming back to me from time to time of a winter's night under the stars. With just a sliver of the new moon off to the west, I remember the stunning brilliance of the Milky Way. I had just learned from a grade-school teacher that this was the edge of the galaxy where we earthlings live. I was astonished; the sense of that night was so wondrous because, for the first time, I was connecting the sight of the starry heavens with the knowledge of galaxies. The perception itself made a lasting impression on me, though there have been times when I have taken the night sky for granted. The wonderment was in my eyes first being opened to what was there, and seeing more than I had ever dreamed could be "up there" and "out there." I was awakening to wonder in nature, and to a basic sense of awe that changed me and my sense of the world.

Such awe in the face of natural forces is still available to us. Those who deeply love the natural world rarely lack this sense of wonderment. The created order is indeed awesome in the original sense of the term. "Look, Mommy, there's a falling star!" can still evoke wonder—even if the parent tells the child that it is "a meteor, dear." So our children can still remind us of our first experiences of this natural awe.

Awe of Destruction

But other things are awesome now as well. In our age, the violent and the destructive events often capture our attention more than the natural world around us does. Many of us are far removed from a sense of "created order," but we are all too aware of human-made apocalypse. The image of a mushroom cloud over a populated city is "awesome." God's final judgment is pictured as a nuclear holocaust. The news media continually bring to our attention such horrors as bombings or mass murders or disasters. More and more, we seem to need spectacular shows, bigger light and sound displays to stimulate us toward a kind of awe. This takes us a long way from the world of the psalms, and alienates us from the world of which "How Great Thou Art" sings.

But there is still an awe in the face of death, where life is still held dear. When we must look upon someone—once alive and loved—now dead, we are first struck by the utter stillness of the body. The contrast between what we expect from a living being and what we see in the "unliving" body is enormous. This may be one place where Christian worship still must pause to reflect on limits, and to encounter the unknown mystery of our mortality. Some liturgies, as we shall note, are given over to this encounter—funerals, Ash Wednesday, Good Friday, and themes within the cycles of time, including night prayer, in which sleep is a metaphor for death.

We have much to learn from the ancient prophets. Isaiah's vision in the temple is a reminder that encounter with God is always an opening to wonder and amazement. While few these days would speak of having such a vision, *without* the sense of radical amazement at the reality of God, the liturgy remains domesticated. To come alive to what the liturgy contains and implies we must learn to be attentive to what it is to address and be addressed by the living God. As Abraham Heschel observed: "The way remains closed to those to whom God is less real than a 'consuming fire,' to those who know answers but no wonder."[1]

Worship and Life Connect and Awaken Awe

If we are to recover and deepen our sense of awe it will be in part because we make connections between what happens in worship and our primary pattern of experience in life. Unless we bring to the speaking, the singing, the praying, and the meal our sense of life and death, the liturgies will remain "churchy." The mystery of remembering the long way of mercy will not flourish if the meeting of human pain and joy with the divine offer of grace is reduced to what is merely "handed down." The secret of this recovery is with the nonverbal languages of worship: gesture, music, the visual, the interpersonal interaction.

Discovering the Mystery

Several years ago, I led a retreat with a group of college students on the meaning of the Lord's Supper. In one session I asked them to tell stories about meals they had eaten which were significant memories for them. It took a while before the notion of a "memorable meal" began to emerge. Finally, one rather shy sophomore described a Thanksgiving meal at her grandparents' house. After speaking of the details of the table and the conversation, she quietly added, "and that was the last time I ate with my grandmother and grandfather." There was among us for that remaining hour a great solemnity, a sense of having touched something holy in one another. The act of sharing was itself an entry point into a renewed sense of reverence when we subsequently celebrated a simple Eucharist at the beach house together.

The words of thanksgiving, the gesture of pouring the wine and breaking the bread, the turning to one another in love, and the giving and receiving of the elements was charged with new meaning. Later one said, "I think I know now what we set out to do on the retreat—discover the mystery." I thought immediately of St. Augustine's observation that when we hold out our hands for the Eucharist, it is our own mystery we receive.

We sometimes hear that Christian worship in the common assembly is for the glorification of God and the sanctification of what is human. This is a theological truth, to be sure. But it remains hollow or abstract apart from the sense of meeting to which I am referring.

Intimacy and Otherness

Where is this tent of meeting—this place of encounter? It is wherever something and someone other than ourselves is encountered *in and through* human speech, gesture, song, and ritual action. The biblical tradition holds out the stories of such meetings. Overwhelmingly, the sense of a holy place brings together a Holy Other who is both wholly other and intimately present. In recalling the Hebrew place names we have a sense of this: Bethel, Shechem, the river Jabbok, Mount Horeb. We also recall the prophet Isaiah's astounding vision in the temple (Isaiah 6). Names of places recall awesome meetings with God: the burning bush, the crossing of the Red Sea, the mount of transfiguration, and the vision of a new Jerusalem. But the Christian tradition of worship does not stop there. There is the witness of Jesus who speaks of worship not on a holy mountain nor in places made by human hands—rather, of God in all times and places.

We move between "It is a fearful thing to fall into the hands of the living God" and "Come, my beloved." On the one hand, we remain mortal creatures distant from our divine source; on the other, we are those whom Jesus calls no longer slaves but "friends." We are both. And our worship must form us in the awareness of both. But to express both to God takes time and place and a book of memory. It takes continuity of stories, and discontinuity in our experience. Christian liturgy flourishes when the contrast and connection between reverence and love is kept alive; when we are rooted in time, place, and memory continually renewed.

Pondering the Source of Awe

The Holy Other who is intimately present—this is the source of any sense of awe before God. This sense is never the simple thrill of grandeur, though such experience gives us fit images and clues for thinking of God. No, just as in my childhood encounter with the starry, starry night, we come to see, hear, taste the presence of God in a qualitatively different way because of the particular stories and songs and teachings about the Holy One our common worship offers.

Seekers will come to the edge of this and find the "strange world" of the Bible an invitation and perhaps an obstacle. But there is no way around the need for the specific character of God's Word. That Word in the Scripture, proclamation, and sacrament keeps stretching us—seekers and "settled believers" alike. Worship well-grounded in the whole Bible continually invites us to ponder the mystery of God's ways just as Mary pondered in her heart the awesome work of God.

Reconnecting Real Life and Worship

What are the points of connection between how we worship in our gathered assemblies and the reawakening of awe and reverence in everyday life? Five places where patterns of experience intersect with specific liturgies or elements in worship come to mind. I have drawn these from my participation in retreat groups and worship services in a wide range of congregations during the past three years.

Several of the occasions when people have told me of a reawakened sense of awe and wonder had to do with the grandeur and intricacy of the natural world. I have already alluded to this. In several congregations this has taken the form of worship on retreat, where the rhythm of night and day, sunrise and sunset, work, rest, and play have set the environment for worship. As we restore some sense of shared common life—rising, praying, eating, studying, and playing together—the psalms of praise and thanksgiving that speak of sun, moon, stars, and the "watches of the night" (Psalm 134, for example) begin to make sense as our actual language of prayer. To awaken the dawn with singing praise is to reenter the psalmist's experience.

The second point of connection has come when people have been exposed to current knowledge of the vastness of the universe, and the limits of our own perspectives. In one case, a pastor had referred to recent theories of the universe, not as a challenge to doctrines of creation, but as wonderment about how little we know. The prayers that morning were also directed toward our gaining wisdom from God concerning our role in the whole created order, reminding us that God created both the heavens and the earth. The hymn of the morning was "God of the Sparrow God of the Whale," sung by the youth choir in dialogue with the congregation.

A third occasion for the connection between real experience and what we do in worship is the funeral service. A local church I visited recently had come

27

through two weeks in which six members, both young and old, had died, of lingering illness and by sudden accident. Through the actual ministries of various families and the "grief team" of laity and clergy, that congregation rediscovered the connection between what it means to belong to one another by baptism into Jesus Christ and the way in which the whole church could grieve and celebrate their friends and beloved ones in the face of the mystery of our mortality. One person said, "I'm so glad we have the new Service of Death and Resurrection—it is *real*, and it rings true to my sorrow and to my faith."

A fourth point of connection is the opposite of awe in the face of death—it is joy over the newborn. In one church I know, the birth of a child or grandchild to church members is an occasion for special prayers of blessing. At Oakhurst Baptist Church in Atlanta, a long-time member receives and physically lifts up the child in an African style of blessing. Every time I witness that, and the surrounding of those parents and grandparents by the song and prayer of that congregation, I realize how extraordinary the grace of God is—that a human community can rejoice so in one another, and especially in the sign of new life in their midst.

All of us, in one way or another, seek a blessing. In fact, many persons, both outside and inside our churches, search throughout their adult lives for a blessing they may never have received in childhood. In a service of healing and blessing, I have seen the remarkable truth dawn, as hands are laid upon those who present themselves, that God is ready to give a blessing. Healing services, which may include prayer and song and laying on of hands, for either physical or mental healing, and especially for the healing of brokenness in relationships, are a fifth occasion for wonder and awe. For the heart of Christian worship is the promise that Jesus Christ stands in our midst, ready to receive us, to heal and give blessing.

These are but five ways in which specific aspects of our ongoing worship patterns—fellowship, preaching, celebrating funerals, celebrating new births, and praying for healing—can awaken us to the grace of God, freely offered. These are the points of intersection in which liturgy comes to life, and our lives can be brought to liturgy.

No Longer a Stranger

In the spring of 1985, I took part in a seminar on orthodoxy in the Ecumenical Center at Bossey, just outside Geneva, Switzerland. Within our gathering we discovered students and pastors from Germany, France, Ethiopia, Great Britain, Russia, and Romania, and two of us from the United States. That year, the Eastern Orthodox churches celebrated Holy Week and Easter the very next week following the Western churches. All of us were invited to the Center at Chambezy to participate in the liturgies throughout the week. Each evening of Holy Week we attended one of the various congregations there. Among these were a large, French-speaking Greek Orthodox parish, an expatriate Russian Orthodox group, and a small peasant Romanian church, complete with its iconography on the outside walls of the building.

On Easter Eve we attended the Easter Vigil, which was being celebrated in each of the congregations. Shortly after midnight, as each liturgy came to its conclusion, we all began to emerge from the churches, spilling out into the clear night air. Bells were ringing from each church, and the people began singing in several languages, "Christ is risen, Christ is risen!" Some picked up the ancient song, "Christ is risen from the dead, trampling down death by death, and to those in the tombs, bestowing life!" It was as though the whole world had gathered in that one place. It was as though the entire cosmos was shouting, and joining us in the song of resurrection. It was a supreme moment in which I was reacquainted with awe and wonder—and in which I was connected with those people, most of whom I had never met, in a way that shall follow me my life long. I can still hear and see echoes of that Easter Vigil in many other places of worship. All the languages met each other. No longer a stranger, I stood at the very center of the world, where God has chosen to reveal life to us all in the form of the crucified and risen Christ.

It was as though all were now kin to me. Despite our remarkable differences of language and culture and style, we were drawn together in the hospitality of God, even though, as a non-Orthodox, the pain of not being able to share Eucharist was there for me. But the breakfast which followed lasted well on toward the dawn. This is the sense so missing for many of us—the sense of being at the very place where God has chosen to be revealed.

Discerning Fresh Accents of Awe

There are a number of new hymns which speak in fresh accents about the places where God is revealed.

One which has quickly become a favorite across gen-
erational lines is Jaroslav Vajda's "God of the Sparrow
God of the Whale." This is truly a contemporary way
of expressing what belongs to the deepest biblical
tradition:

God of the sparrow God of the whale
God of the swirling stars
How does the creature say Awe
How does the creature say Praise

God of the earthquake God of the storm
God of the trumpet blast
How does the creature cry Woe
How does the creature cry Save

God of the rainbow God of the cross
God of the empty grave
How does the creature say Grace
How does the creature say Thanks

God of the hungry God of the sick
God of the prodigal
How does the creature say Care
How does the creature say Life

God of the neighbor God of the foe
God of the pruning hook
How does the creature say Love
How does the creature say Peace

God of the ages God near at hand
God of the loving heart
How do your children say Joy
How do your children say Home[2]

Here is a bold and surprising list of images for God,
with a corresponding list of questions we must ask. I
have found many people coming to love this hymn,

finding it gathering more meaning for them the more they sing it. So I discover a new way to ask the question: "How does the creature say 'Awe'?"

I am convinced that the wonder, the mystery, and the awe of God are still present. We are the ones too often absent. What lies before us we miss. As Gerard Manley Hopkins said of beauty:

> These things, these things were here and but the be-
> holder
>   Wanting: which two when they once meet,
> The heart rears wings bold and bolder
>   And hurls for him, O half hurls earth for him off
>   under his feet.[3]

Worship can form us, every aspect of our lives, in such a habit of beholding. Charles Wesley's great hymn "Love Divine, All Loves Excelling" finds us "lost in wonder, love, and praise." In season and out of season, we are to rehearse such wonder and prepare for such awe. But the end of this is beatitude, blessedness in the presence of God. This is when we learn again to offer our lives—all we have and all we are—in adoration of God. It is certainly something of what Paul had in mind in his Letter to the Romans when he said that we should offer ourselves, our souls and bodies, in a sacrifice of praise and thanksgiving to God.

Where may we meet this wonder and awe of God? Both in daily life and in liturgy. Or, perhaps we can meet God in the liturgy because of what is given in daily life; and we can recognize what is given in daily life because of what we continually rehearse and receive in the liturgy.

CHAPTER TWO

The Sense of Delight

◆

'Tis the gift to be simple, 'tis the gift to be free,
'Tis the gift to come down where we ought to be;
And when we find ourselves in the place just right,
'Twill be in the valley of love and delight.

—TRADITIONAL, "SIMPLE GIFTS"

So often we miss the essentials. Not only in our daily lives are we unaware of what is right before us, but also in our gatherings for worship. In our concern to do what is expected, and in our routine habits, we settle for our duty. Thus we miss one of the most essential features of vital worship: sheer delight—delight in God, in one another, and in the very means by which common life is graced. Obligation, custom, and "the way we've always done it" obscure the delight. Hence we suffer a diminished liturgy and life together.

The disarming simplicity of the Shaker song, "Simple Gifts," reminds us of what is so easily neglected. The Shakers were certainly not known for elaborate Christian liturgy! Yet they took a wondrous delight in their assembled dancing. In various drawings we have of their meetings we see the seemingly odd, stylized forward and backward turning, turning of their dance—the men on one side, the women on the other. Here we find a ritual dance which gave them the freedom and the delight about which they sang.

Isaac Watts's paraphrase of Psalm 147, even with its eighteenth-century language, reminds me of our theme:

> Praise ye the Lord; 'tis good to raise
> our hearts and voices in his praise:
> his nature and his works invite
> to make this duty our delight.[1]

Likewise, the psalmist in the songs of praise links rejoicing in God with the delight of the divine presence: "How lovely is your dwelling place, O LORD of hosts!"(Psalm 84:1). Worshiping God in the "beauty of holiness" generates both wonder and delight even while being commanded by God. The marriage of duty and delight lies at the heart of biblical worship. We are to praise and bless God even when we don't feel like it, only to discover, in doing so, that God is our first love and the wellspring of all enjoyment.

This theme is echoed once again in Erik Routley's twentieth-century hymn, "For Musicians":

> In praise of God meet duty and delight,
> angels and creatures, men and spirits bless'd;
> in praise is earth transfigured by the sound
> and sight of heaven's everlasting feast.[2]

All creatures, indeed all of heaven and earth are gathered in this image of worship. In particular, the sight and sound of the heavenly banquet in the celebration of Holy Communion is the chief occasion of delight. There is delight also at the awesome promise of earth's transformation implied by the Eucharist.

I picture a congregation I know in which a woman confined to a motorized wheelchair is a regular participant in the Sunday gathering. There is certainly pain and limitation in her life. But once, at the end of a particularly festive liturgy in which children had a role, she came down the aisle to receive communion. After the final blessing and hymn we happened to be in line together to greet the clergy. With a broad smile and eyes sparkling beneath the rim of her Easter hat she said to me, "Didn't we dance today?"

That remark suddenly awakened in me an awareness of what we had just experienced. I had been preoccupied with other matters and, quite frankly, had not been very present. But she brought back to me with her sense of delight in the music and readings, and in the sheer ability to be present and to move to and from the altar, the "event" of worship to which I had been so dull. In her disability she participated and perceived that we all, mostly able-bodied, had danced and sung together unto God.

Practicing Delight-Taking

Such an experience reveals a deeper aspect of our worship. When we bring a sense of gratitude, joy, and delight to common worship, the celebration of the gospel in word, song, and sacrament begins to reveal its own joy and delight. We are present in worship as living reminders for one another as well. Over time the meeting about the book, the font, and the table of the Lord offers us the possibility of enjoyment of the divine life given to us in human form. We can never quite predict which specific dimension of the liturgy—readings, music, gestures, movements, ritual actions, the faces and voices of those around us—will occasion such delight. Ideally, as we shall see, all parts of the liturgy should work together. We are still being formed in the sense of the possibility of receiving, as the psalmist says, a "greater joy than when their grain and new wine abound" (Psalm 4:7 NIV).

Alongside our hopes and fears, hurts and longings, we must learn to bring a need for wonder and gladness, for awe and delight. When we are not encouraged to do so, and when we never practice delight-taking, the world itself is dulled and is far less hospitable to being surprised by joy. At the heart of Christian worship is the astounding claim that God takes delight in the whole creation, in the movement from death to life, and in the human awakening to grace in everyday life. In this way, Christian liturgy is a kind of rehearsal for living life at fuller stretch before God.

C. S. Lewis, in *Reflections on the Psalms,* muses on why praise and delight in God go together, and why they are essential. At first disturbed by the notion that God demands a kind of "perpetual eulogy," Lewis gradually realized that all deep enjoyment flows into praise unless someone or something deliberately prevents it. Thus, lovers delight in and praise their loved ones, citizens their heroines and heroes, and religious believers their saints and holy forebears. Lewis concludes that the psalmist's enjoyment of praise is simply what all healthy human beings do when we address that which we most truly care about. What we adore and revere we praise and delight in. "We delight to praise what we enjoy because the praise not merely expresses but completes the enjoyment; it is its appointed consummation."[3]

In that classic piece of Protestant confession, the Westminster Catechism, the very first question asks,

"What is the chief end of man?" That is, what is the purpose for which human beings are created? And the answer? "To glorify God, and to enjoy him forever." There is the point without qualification. None of us, and no human community can find our best being without the glorification of our creator and the sense of delight in all that God has created and offered. If this is not found in our gathered assemblies for worship, it is difficult to know where we might learn it, for at the heart of the public worship of God is the story of God's continual creating and redeeming intent: to give life, and to give it in abundance.

To complete our praise of God in enjoyment of God and all that is created in love, and to express and complete the delight in life before God in our praise: this is the double truth of authentic Christian worship. It is also profoundly relevant to an age of cynicism and consumerist self-absorption. The cynical attitude teaches us that everything has a string attached to it. Worship looks beyond that to see that our very existence is a gift freely given. The prophetic vision of God's will also teaches us that God is not mocked by the cynic, nor can the "power of God" be bought and consumed. The double truth of authentic Christian worship restores us to gratitude, and leads us toward self-giving for others.

Participation in Worship as Participation in Life

Attentive participation in the worship life of the Christian community is related to a way of being in the world. Liturgical participation can heighten our sense of joy in the details of life and in the mystery of being related to God and to one another as kin. This is reminiscent of the Sioux Indian saying: "All are kin to me."

And yet, so often Christian worship has led to anything but this sense of life. We have often experienced the worshiping community to exclude others not like us, and our prayers reflect our own immediate self-preoccupations. Sermons have often tended to reduce the Scripture to a series of moral teachings and special oracles. Where is the delightful singing the whole range of the glory and holiness of God? Where are the vibrant celebrations—baptisms, the Lord's Supper, Love Feasts, healing services, and morning and evening prayers—that are hospitable, and open to the mystery of the whole range of God's grace?

These are not easy questions, and no one general answer is possible for the wide variety of social and cultural contexts of worshiping communities. But some reminders of essential theological dimensions of the sense of delight and of specific practices we can cultivate may be helpful.

Among the most central aspects of Christian worship are praise and thanksgiving. If "liturgy" is really the "work of the people of God" in the continuing remembrance and life of God in the world, then the remembrance itself must be full-blooded. This is why worship is starved when there is no accompanying Scripture study, and so little Scripture is read, sung, and prayed in our common assemblies. When only one lesson is read, and it is never clearly connected with what is preached, prayed, or sung, is it any wonder that the assembly loses a sense of its own larger history? When people complain that too much reading of

Scripture is boring, perhaps the connection with praise and thanksgiving and deep memory is already missing. But the problem may also be the *way* the Bible is presented: the presenter may be ill-prepared, or the text may be poorly read (or sung)!

Suppose that worship can be freshly imaged as the common action of presenting our lives in response to and in union with the ongoing prayer and deeds of Christ. If worship is initiated by the God who creates and redeems in love, and who seeks the creatures to delight in a life of gratitude and thanksgiving, then why should our liturgies lack those very qualities?

Life is brought to holiness and delight by a continual rehearsal of thanks. Again and again the psalms sing, "Bless the LORD, O my soul," and "let every thing that breathes praise the LORD." This is our basic vocation as God's people—to stand in the midst of life and to remember God in praise, blessing, and thanksgiving. But this is also the doorway to delight, the window to joy.

The Realities of Delight East of Eden

Sadly, the relations between being grateful and expressing that gratitude and delight must also stand the test of pain and disappointment. East of Eden, no one can sustain delight-taking all the time—at least in the sense of being on a natural "high." To live attentively and intensely is also to suffer. Some pleasures and enjoyments are episodes which last only a short while. A child wins a prize at the carnival and dances and shouts for joy, "I've won, I'm so happy!" But, the wise parent, in acknowledging the child's good pleasure, also knows that it will soon fade. Part of growing up is learning to tell the difference between the childish delights of good luck and the deeper, longer lasting enjoyments of something well done or of a love cultivated over time.

This is simply to observe that in liturgy, as in life, we do well to tell the difference between short-term episodes of pleasure and the deeper, more permanent sources of joy and delight. Christian worship speaks, sings, prays, and enacts the source of all created enjoyment in the divine life. What's more, vital worship grants us a gift of our own life transformed in the promises of God. The mystery of our life hid with Christ in God is sounded and offered back to us in the praying, the singing, the elements of bread and wine, the water, the oil, and the laying on of hands. When worship is faithful to its true subject—God incarnate and Spirit-giving—and relevant to our restlessness for God, it will restore us to joy and delight.

When worship touches down in the wellsprings of life, we sense that it is finally the overflow of God's delight in us and in the whole created order which is primary. The divine creativity has made, and the incarnate God of human history is redeeming, *this world*, despite all our joyless neglect and life-denying.

For a long time I had difficulty understanding Paul's admonition to "Rejoice always . . . give thanks in all circumstances" (1 Thessalonians 5:16, 18a). I kept thinking that this was simply impossible. Not all circumstances are joyful, let alone enjoyable! This seemed to me a piece of irrelevant piety. I was offended by easy, "ultra-bright" Christian behavior. But after considerable life experience with pain and complexity, it occurred to me that God is not asking to be thanked *for* the pain or *for* the seasons of difficulty. Rather, in continuing the practice of gratitude to God we are reminding ourselves of the steadfast love of God in and through all circumstances. This practice, repeated again and again in Christian worship, is perhaps the most relevant way of being present to both joy and sorrow.

One of the occasions in which this deeper sense of delight in God came to me was in a Quaker meeting. In the deepening silence of the gathering I became increasingly aware of the changing light-fall in the room. It was a day of stormy, threatening clouds with intervals of brilliant sun. As the alternating patches of sunlight and shadow fell on the faces of those gathered, it was as though God was showing me what the whole sweep of Scripture speaks: the rain falls on the just and the unjust, the pain and the joy are always mingled. These faces of friends, and of those I did not know, were illuminated parables of the grace of God. In those moments I was filled with a nearly unbearable sense of gratitude. Afterwards, what I heard in the conversation, both casual and serious, was a deeper echo of Christ's presence in the world and in my life.

The same sort of thing has occurred in many a celebration of the Eucharist. Often, while persons are coming forward to commune at various places in the chapel where I serve as organist, I see the whole world converging in this simple meal. Whenever there are people of many different races and backgrounds, this mystery intensifies. In sharing this with students, I have often been referred to as a "local mystic." But the more I talk with those who have intentionally developed a more attentive way of celebrating and participating in the holy meal, the more I hear others speak of this living image. And the more I listen to them, the more I understand this as a common language which shapes and expresses the experience of everyday life. The breaking of bread is less casual, and the faces and hands of others who have fed and been fed by Christ seem more graceful.

We touch here upon the deepest source of delight and joy human beings can have: the sense of the sacredness of life, and how it is sustained by the Holy One of all creation.

So why do we settle for so little? In part it is because we bring so little to Christian worship. There is so much difference between coming to be entertained—to simply receive a shot of grace or good advice for the coming week—and bringing all of our life to the table of the Word and the meal. To gather in the name of Jesus to praise God and to hear with delight and awe what God speaks and does in our midst is to come to the place where duty and delight embrace. If we should discover in such a place God's way with us, then it will be in wonder and praise. Would this not send us to live with a deeper delight and gladness than if we only celebrate ourselves as we already are?

But then, we may also settle for so little because we bring too much with us: cluttered lives, a thousand distractions, and our habitual images of ourselves. Christian liturgy does not force us; we are invited and thus must be prepared. There is considerable virtue in the practice of making confession before receiving Eucharist. This is not because God does not accept sinners at the table, but simply because preparing to worship God gives us an opportunity to make connections between how we live and how we shall worship God. When invited to someone's special dinner party, do we not prepare in some special way? If we take it for granted or show up late with our minds and hearts elsewhere, the dinner and conversation will not be engaging. We risk alienating our hosts, or disappointing them in all the preparation they lavished for our coming with other guests. So it is with Christian liturgy.

good example for news).

Keeping Delight and Joy Alive

One of the ways the freshness of joy and delight is offered to us is through the keeping of certain feasts and seasons. Some days, such as Easter and Pentecost, Christmas and Epiphany, are dedicated to the remembrance of the great things God has done. But this freshness is available in the ordinary Sundays as well—in the sheer grace of gathering about the book of memory and the table of ongoing grace, and in the midst of a community praying for the whole world with Christ.

When the worship service is treated primarily as a forum in which to give advice and to entertain with episodes of feeling, we may well lose this sense of delight in God. The deeper relevance is found in the sustained stories, songs, and offering of Christ to the world in the ordinary means of love. This is the long memory of God practiced in true worship. The paradox of delight in God is found only when our worship enables us to weep with those who weep and to rejoice with those who rejoice. When the connection between the forms and patterns of liturgy and the actual pathos of life is dulled or forgotten, there is neither awe nor ecstatic delight.

Experiencing the Complete Palette of Delight

We have spoken of that sense of delight which springs from the divine play in creation and redemption. There are many images of this in the music of the Christian tradition. A centuries-old text sings:

> To-morrow shall be my dancing day:
> I would my true love did so chance
> To see the legend of my play,
> To call my true love to my dance:
>
> *Refrain:* Sing O my love, O my love, my love, my love;
> This have I done for my true love.[4]

It is surprising to many that the whole range of Jesus' birth, life, death, and resurrection should all be included in the dancing. But dancing is that part of the tradition which can best express God's wisdom—the playful, creative aspect of God's activity. This aspect of God, referred to in Proverbs, came to be associated in the early church with Jesus as both Word and incarnate mystery.

A more contemporary strand of this deeper delight-taking is found in Sydney Carter's well-known song of Jesus, "Lord of the Dance":

> I danced in the morning
> When the world was begun,
> And I danced in the moon
> And the stars and the sun,
> And I came down from heaven
> And I danced on the earth,
> At Bethlehem
> I had my birth.

Chorus: Dance, then, wherever you may be,
I am the Lord of the Dance, said he,
And I'll lead you all, wherever you may be,
And I'll lead you all in the Dance, said he.

I danced for the scribe
And the Pharisee,
But they would not dance
And they wouldn't follow me.
I danced for the fishermen,
For James and John—
They came with me
And the dance went on.

I danced on the Sabbath
And I cured the lame;
The holy people
Said it was a shame.
They whipped and they stripped
And they hung me on high,
And they left me there
On a cross to die.

I danced on a Friday
When the sky turned black—
It's hard to dance
With the devil on your back.
They buried my body
And they thought I'd gone,
But I am the dance,
And I still go on.

They cut me down
And I leapt up high;
I am the life
That'll never, never die;
I'll live in you

If you'll live in me—
I am the Lord
Of the Dance, said he.[5]

These are but two examples expressing the song of delight for all creation—the hosts of heaven and all earthly creatures, great and small. It is the first and final vocation of heaven and earth to glorify the divine source of life. Christian worship flourishes when this is recognized, planned for, and celebrated well over time. It begins with linking the reading of the goodness of creation and the glory of God in Christ with the ongoing song of the faithful. The psalms of praise wait for us to rediscover this. The biblical canticles, from the song of Miriam and Moses in Exodus 15:1-18, 21 to Mary's song in Luke 1:47-55, to the great hymns of praise which punctuate the concluding chapters of Revelation, are all part of this language of delight in God. When these are neglected, our worship is undernourished, and our sense of being in the world is diminished.

The awakening of this godly delight is to be found in every dimension of worship: what we hear, see, smell, taste, touch, and sign with our movements. Some of us may need to learn again from the children's delight, from the hands and faces of those who greet us and exchange Christ's peace, from honoring our elders, from the textures and colors of the changing year, from the flowers and the fresh-baked bread and from the sounds of instruments, voices, and words lovingly and prayerfully spoken. When the whole range of our senses is activated by the Word and sacramental signs of God, life comes to worship, and worship comes alive.

The Heart of Worship and Delight: The Heavenly Fiesta

The great biblical image of the feast for all peoples lies at the heart of all our worship—whether on great feast days or on the low-ebb Sundays. The celebrations of many Hispanic and Latino communities, with their bright colors, processions, and dances, provide images of what worship can be—a heavenly fiesta of Word, song, and holy meal. To this eternal source of delight in God's unfailing promise we must return in the final chapter, to see how delight and hope may embrace.

It is easy in North American consumerist culture to confuse delight with entertainment or the frivolity of mere self-expression. Delight in the things of God is never passive or self-indulgent. The pleasure and joy of being *alive* to creation deepens gratitude. The "holy play"[6] of which we speak is not the celebration of our class values, but of God's claim upon all of life in Christ. This holy play requires discipline, and a long memory. This holy play asks of us vulnerability to grace and to one another. This holy play invites us to a profound trust that God has created us to delight in the gift of life. Here liturgy takes our work and play, our suffering and rejoicing into a new "lightness of being" precisely by joining us to Jesus' liturgy—and hence into his dying and rising in our world.

CHAPTER THREE

The Sense of Truth

◆

From the cowardice that dares not face new truth,
from the laziness that is contented with half-truth,
from the arrogance that thinks it knows all truth,
Good Lord, deliver me. Amen.

—PRAYER FROM KENYA

This prayer has not let me go since I first discovered it in *The United Methodist Hymnal* (no. 597). It said then and still says what we need to pray daily. The words are direct and arresting. They cut through our politeness with God. Sooner or later, all praise and thanksgiving, all that we preach, sing, and pray must come to the court of truth.

The Elusiveness of Truth

Dishonesty with God and with one another dominates much of our social and personal life. It should not be surprising that truthfulness is hard to come by in politics. But this is so in the patterns of church life as well, and so too in our liturgies. When someone says of our preaching or of our pastoral prayers that they don't "ring true," it goes straight to the heart. It is relatively rare to hear this at the church door on Sunday morning, but for many persons this is what is at stake in their worship experience. All too often this disappointment is kept private. All the more urgent, then, that we should ask here: Why do worship services not ring true to people, some of whom attend Sunday upon Sunday?

We can, of course, dismiss the question quickly by saying that the church can't please all the people all the time. Or, we may say conveniently that there are many different styles; not everyone in this particular congregation appreciates our way of doing things. I hear this again and again with respect to hymns and service music. We may simply maneuver around the question of truthfulness by reducing it to a matter of taste. Or, more recently, worship leaders are likely to observe that different age groups, social groups, or psychological types will simply react differently to different kinds of music and liturgical styles. As a general observation about human beings, this is certainly so.

Getting to the Real Truth

It is not possible here to discuss the problems with a reduction of truthfulness to taste, or with the troublesome use of easy typecasting of groups. The question of relevance is important. Whether or not a particular form or style of worship speaks to the needs of particular groups within and outside our churches should not be dismissed. In this chapter I want to raise a set of issues which are prior to cultural relevance, but which also follow from current strategic efforts about how to reach human beings through Christian worship. These concerns cluster around the adequacy of our worship: Who is God? And what is required for our worship to address God truthfully about ourselves and our world? For it is possible to be relevant and yet inadequate to the mystery of faith. It is also possible to set forth dogmatic truths which do not elicit a living faithfulness in worship or in common life.

Christian liturgy, whether "high" or "low," storefront or cathedral, is first and last praising, adoring, and thanking God in, with, and through Jesus Christ in the power of the Spirit. If we say, as in the previous chapters, that this requires a sense of both awe and delight, then the question of truthfulness is in order. Can we make the mistake of hiding behind our praise and thanks rather than being radically open to God through such activity? What happens when all we have is a steady diet of routine thanksgiving, and find ourselves covering over the hurt, the confusion, and the struggle to face other aspects of our personal and communal lives in the presence of God? The answer to the first question is "yes." The answer to the second is "praise and thanksgiving are thereby diminished." It may even be that when we cover over the truth about ourselves and our world by saying "Lord, Lord," we deceive ourselves and presume upon God.

If the first question of the Westminster Catechism, "What is the chief end of humankind?" is answered "to glorify and to enjoy God forever," we cannot worship very long before we must ask why we do not do so! The answer to this challenging question is: because we have turned away from God to our own devices and desires.

The gap between what "ought to be" and what "is" sets up a permanent tension for all Christian worship which seeks to be faithful. On the one hand, we are called to offer continual praise and thanksgiving. Such a response to the self-giving of God involves remembering the whole story of God in Christ—from creation, through covenants, prophecy, and the incarnation, to the promised fulfillment of all things in Christ. On the other hand, such remembering gathers up who we are and what the world has become in the sight of God. This means that if we are to hear the Word and receive the life God offers we must also come to terms with the truth about ourselves. Acknowledging God involves encountering the truth about the human story. This is the awesome image Isaiah gives us as part of his vision of the Holy One in the temple. In seeing the vision, he confesses, "Woe is me! . . . for I am a man of unclean lips, and I live among a people of unclean lips" (Isaiah 6:5). So a permanent tension marks the flow of Christian worship through our lives; acknowledging and praising God explores and continually reveals the difference between the Creator and the creatures, between who God in Christ is and who we are.

Confession of our sinfulness is only one dimension of the sense of truth, as we shall soon see. Yet it is crucial, for without self-knowledge our praise and thanks can become distorted. Truth in our inner selves and in our relationships is also necessary to becoming human. To address God is to be addressed by God. So God's holiness and justice and love illuminate the landscape of human history as well as our own personal character. Any genuine sense of truth in our gathered assemblies asks that we give time, place, word, and ritual care to the discovery of the truth about ourselves. Who are we in God's presence? The Christian faith replies, we are saints and sinners, creatures of intense worth to God, yet alienated from the source of our life with one another. So thanksgiving, praise, and living memory are essential to Christian worship and to our humanity; but so is coming to the truth about ourselves and our worship. We come to the truth when liturgy comes to its senses.

From Routinization to Transformation

It is one thing to ask with Pilate, "What is truth?" It is another to learn, over time, to speak and live the truth in love. Christian theology claims that certain things are true of God, the world, and human history. But, again, these truths remain strange and remote from daily life when our worship does not allow us to experience them. Words about the truth are not enough: the truth must be embodied in a real-life community. Why else would Jesus have said, "Not everyone who says to me, 'Lord, Lord,' will enter the kingdom of heaven"? (Matthew 7:21). "Be doers of the word, and not merely hearers" (James 1:22)—this we have heard, but find it difficult. Could it be that our sense of worship itself prevents us? Could it be that we have allowed worship to become too "wordy" and too routine to open for us a transformed way of living?

There are, of course, words that help, and words that encourage. I am particularly grateful for the inclusion of the prayer "For True Singing" in the recent *United Methodist Hymnal* (no. 69):

Glorious God, source of joy and righteousness,
enable us as redeemed and forgiven children
    evermore to rejoice in singing your praises.
Grant that what we sing with our lips

we may believe in our hearts,
and what we believe in our hearts
   we may practice in our lives;
so that being doers of the Word and not hearers only,
   we may receive everlasting life;
through Jesus Christ our Lord. *Amen.*

Even though these are "just words," they are powerful because they are both poetic and biblical, and they humbly invite us. They keep us focused on God's grace, while permitting us to overhear the truth about ourselves. This prayer reminds us, as we pray it together, that our singing already is an act which opens our intentions and actions to the grace of God.

A surprise is contained here: we will know the truth, and the truth will set us free, only when our actual life "sings." There are many in our churches whose faithful service sings the truth beyond the hymns and songs of worship. This is why we are touched by a new generation of children innocently singing, "I would be true, for there are those who trust me."[1] And we pray that their lives will never lose touch with basic trust when childhood fades into adolescence and the complexities beyond.

Worship in Spirit and Truth as Shared Life in Christ

What is it to worship God "in spirit and in truth"? The answer to this question goes beyond the current culture-wars debate about elitist versus popular styles. In fact we cannot answer the question with any standardized formula. It is a question about spirituality, about the character of shared life in Christ. It forces us to examine both the truth about what our hymns, prayers, sermons, and sacraments say and do, and the truthfulness of our life in the Holy Spirit of God. Faithfulness to the truth of God's self-communication in Jesus and truthfulness in our soul and social relations is not easy.

Truthfulness is risky for us who wish to remain polite with God and nice to one another. It does not make things easier to live in a culture where forgetfulness and deception have become a way of life. The emergence in politics of "spin doctors"—politicians' aides who make sure certain actions, statements, and images of their clients receive the most favorable, if not most factual, interpretation—is a symptom of this; but all too often such "doctoring" has invaded our images of worship as well. We know too well the practice of slight dishonesty in our gatherings, and how we then take it out on one another behind one another's backs. We know too well the easy labeling of "conservative" and "liberal" and the opposition-bashing that follows. We know too well how genuine differences in our approaches to worship become obstacles rather than opportunities to learn from one another when we presume to know exactly what constitutes "evangelical" versus "catholic" or "sacramental" Christianity.

These matters have a profound effect on our present struggle for clarity about worship "in spirit and in truth." Even more sobering, however, is how gossip turns to backbiting and recrimination. Dislike of others, never checked by speaking and listening honestly, turns to scapegoating and falsehood. So we in the church make peace with prejudices and with fear of "the other." As one woman who had experienced the sting of rumors about her circulating in the congregation said to me, "I thought the church could at least be a place of modest truth-telling." It was the hurt she experienced there following her having brought a gay friend to visit that finally drove her from worshiping with that congregation.

Honesty at All Costs?

All this sounds like a call for honesty at all costs. Yet pastoral discretion and spiritual friendship know better than to think truth and truthfulness are simply honesty standing alone. There is also mutual respect and a sense of timeliness for speaking about matters and praying in the whole congregation about them. Christian worship is not and cannot be the same as a no-holds-barred therapy session. The sense of truth we seek in common worship must keep company with compassion and with restraint before God. When our liturgies are truthful, they keep reorienting us to our source, and to the God who wishes to speak to us the truth about us and our world. Yet this is always aimed at healing, liberation, and reconciliation.

This means that honesty is not enough. Honesty must always keep company with the divine humility. Here the honesty of Jesus is our model; he spoke with disarming directness but always out of deep compassion, even when righteous anger flashed. We can be brutally honest about something that may turn out to be false. But dishonesty and living out of rumor will eventually distort our prayer and praise. The scribes and Pharisees did not quite grasp this, but the sinners did; hence the parable of the publican and the sinner at prayer in the temple.

To speak truthfully to God and one another is a social grace, essential to faithful liturgy. But such a capacity requires hearing and receiving the truth about ourselves and our world. This is why our worship is diminished so long as we do not have a way to express lamentation, confession, and pleas for forgiveness. Without lamentation, our praise is domesticated; without acknowledgment of our sin and provision for experienced forgiveness, our prophecy is fruitless. Equally important is the provision of truthful witness to what God has done and is doing. Let us turn to three fundamental reforms that are called for in our liturgical practices in the contemporary church. These, I contend, are part of how we may restore and deepen the sense of truth in our worship: lamentation, confession, and testimony.

Deepening Truthfulness in Worship by Lamentation, Confession, and Testimony

In her book *Words That Sing,* Gail Ramshaw reminds us that praise and lament are reciprocal in the Christian liturgy: "Praise opens the door for lament, lament always turns back to praise."[2] There are occasional and crucial exceptions, but the prayer of the church is found in this primal rhythm. This is the rhythm of the psalms, it is the rhythm of our life journey, it is the condition of human history. "The praise and lament are two pitches in the same cry, two melodic lines in the same song."[3] Think, for example, of Francis of Assisi's "Canticle of Brother Son," written in a harsh winter the year before his death in 1225. Nearly blind and in physical pain, he sings of "our sister, gentle death, waiting to hush our latest breath." But even death is caught up in the praise of God by sun and moon, water and fire, storm and all things living.

We need not go past the biblical psalms to see the intimate relationship of speaking truthfully to God of suffering and pain, and yet always moving back to praise and thanksgiving. Perhaps the most searing example is Psalm 22, a fragment of which Jesus cries out in lamentation from the cross—"My God, my God, why have you forsaken me!" Yet Jesus knew full well that the psalm ends in trust and praise, even in the midst of extreme anguish and pain.

Lamentation. For the most part, our worship contains a great many hymns of praise. A sense of liveliness in worship is often recovered with the use of many "praise choruses" in some churches. This, coupled with the rediscovery of "sung Scripture," is a promising development, frequently allowing people to experience a communal joy in singing that is often missing in a steady diet of a narrow range of standard hymns. Yet there lurks a problem here. It is precisely the same problem I see in so much "routine" worship that many are concerned to correct. The problem is the lack of lament.

We have very few occasions that allow us to express honestly and deeply our pain and our anguish. If our churches are to remember and address the cry of the world's peoples and of the creation itself, our worship must have the capacity for grief as well as joy. We know very few hymns that lament, and even these few are often unpopular because of their slow tempo, minor key, or mournful tone. While this may express musical preferences, it also betrays our dis-ease with demanding texts and musical forms—whether from African American, Hispanic, Asian American, or European lineage. We even have trouble using the lamentations of the Bible. Fortunately there are new prayers and hymns being written for our time and place. Brian Wren has written:

> When pain and terror strike by chance,
> with causes unexplained,
> when God seems absent or asleep,
> and evil unrestrained,
> we crave an all-controlling force,
> ready to rule and warn,
> but find, far-shadowed by a cross,
> a child in weakness born.[4]

And, in another hymn, based on the cry of Psalm 88, he sums up the point we are exploring:

> God, give us freedom to lament
> and sing an honest, aching song,
> when Faith is twined with discontent
> and all is empty, wrecked and wrong.

The hymn ends by addressing God, saying,

> We'll walk beside you, come what may,
> to you our hopes and hearts belong,
> and when we've nothing else to say,
> we'll sing an honest, aching song.[5]

Our avoidance of lament has a strange result—it opens a great gulf between our liturgies and our lives. The child still asks, "Why did God let Mommy die?"

We still ask, even as television spews out an endless program of violence and the nightly litany of trouble and death, "Why is the world so filled with pain?" We cry out silently, like the figure in Edvard Munch's famous painting, *The Scream*. Popular music does its own screaming, from rap to alternative rock. Contemporary orchestral and choral music cries out as well. Why is the church so afraid of using what the Bible contains?

There is a difference between raw screaming in anger or anguish and the kind of lament we need to practice in the context of the worship and praise of God. We may cry out in terror, C. S. Lewis once observed, but that only tells us that terror is an earnest emotion.[6] But to cry out to the God who creates and who promises to sustain us through the terror, ah, that is another matter. That is what is missing in much Christian liturgy now. How can we face the truth of human suffering and complicity and injustice without exercising the God-given language of lamentation?

Lament must reenter our experience of worship because it is already built in. The cry of abandonment from the cross is there, part of the story, and part of what we confront if we do justice to Good Friday. It is certainly there on Ash Wednesday when we are given opportunity to lament our sins and turn again to God. "Remember that you are dust" we hear, and then "Repent, and believe the gospel." It is there when we pray honestly for the victims of war, of sudden violence, and when we call to mind our own complicities in the suffering of others. It has to be there if we are to preach (or to prepare ourselves to hear the proclamation) about the prosperity of the wicked and the struggle of the righteous. Above all, it is heard and seen and enacted in the meal at the Lord's table—in the broken bread and the wine poured out from the life of Jesus Christ to us and to all. We need to begin the process of study and experiential education in these primary occasions where lament is present.

I have found several local churches exploring this once again, beginning with the study and the practice of praying the psalms together in the mornings and evenings. The simple rhythm of gathering, singing or reading several psalms together, listening to a biblical lesson, singing a biblical canticle from Luke, praying for the world's needs and for our own, and receiving a blessing can begin to make the psalms real again. The rhythm of lament and praise is clearly present in this form of common prayer.

In studying the meaning of the feasts and seasons of the Christian year, a congregation with which I am familiar has found itself far more alert to the same rhythm of thanksgiving and lament over time. When a tragic accident occurred to a family there, the lay leader said, "We were able to minister as a congregation to the grief and to the slow recovery process because we as a congregation knew the suffering of God more deeply." That is eloquent testimony to what we all need. And it is something we can all begin to practice. When a congregation's worship can speak honestly to the realities of life and connect these to the movements of grace between lament and praise, we will become truly relevant to the needs of others, and perhaps a more authentic evangel for those who do not know the love of God in Christ.

Confession. The second aspect of truth and truthfulness in worship has to do with honesty about sin. Often in crying out about the world's pain and injustice, I find myself brought up short by my own involvement. Is there a place we can go with our own broken promises? Is there a time and a space, and music and prayer, and words which can heal and forgive? Is there "a balm in Gilead to heal the sin-sick soul"?

These are questions we must face again. For too long we have denied the need for real confession and forgiveness, often substituting easy talk about our basic goodness for a truthful understanding of who we are in the presence of God. We have, thank God, learned that not all sin is that of pride or overt action, but we have to learn to name self-hatred and lack of trust as obstacles to relationships with God and neighbor. Redemptive confessing of sin before God is not wallowing in guilt, or endlessly chanting "I'm so terrible." Rather, speaking to God and to one another about what holds us in bondage is liberating. That much therapy knows. But Christian liturgy offers more: grace which frees us to live, to serve, to worship with all that we are—including our shadow side.

In the new baptismal rite of The United Methodist Church, serious questions are asked of those about to be baptized (the parents and sponsors in the case of infants). "Do you renounce the spiritual forces of wickedness, reject the evil powers of this world, and repent of your sin?" This is startling to many of us who find the mention of sin and the powers of evil rather embarrassing. Recently, I overheard someone in a congregation say, "Why do we ask such embarrassing questions of those nice young couples?" The plain fact is that we must find ways in our worship to cease being embarrassed when asked the truth about ourselves and our world. Only by opening up the meaning of such questions outside the room of worship can this process be started. John Wesley certainly realized this in his insistence on spiritual guidance and, above all, on the preparation of the soul for the worship of God.

In this connection, one of the greatest written prayers we have, aside from our Lord's Prayer, is the Collect for Purity. This has been used by many Protestant denominations who have received it from the *Book of Common Prayer*. It has everything to do with truth and truthfulness, and is commended to every congregation to facilitate reflection on our lives in small groups and in sermons:

> Almighty God,
> to you all hearts are open, all desires known,
> and from you no secrets are hidden.
> Cleanse the thoughts of our hearts
> by the inspiration of your Holy Spirit,
> that we may perfectly love you,
> and worthily magnify your holy name,
> through Christ our Lord.
> Amen.[7]

Here, in miniature, is what we must learn again in Christian worship. God is the searcher of hearts, and nothing is hidden from the divine grace.

As a child, I used to think that if God knew everything about me it was a terrible threat. Like some great laser beam in the sky, God was constantly watching for me to make a mistake, have bad thoughts, or harbor secret sins. Many Christians have felt this way, especially those trained in the wrath and judgment of God. But as I grow older, I find a deep comfort in this truth about God. As the complexities of life accumulate—my losses and joys, my good and bad intentions—it is good to know that someone, somewhere, knows all of this.

Confession is a prayer that reminds me that God knows all this and yet seeks to breathe into me a spirit of love and hope. Best of all, the God to whom this is addressed knows our humanity, and has the power to release us from the tyranny of guilt and sinful self-deception. This is healing. This is necessary to the spirit of Christian liturgy. Once again, the text lies before us; the bringing of our life to it requires hospitality to the truth.

Testimony. Having spoken of the need to recover honest lamentation and authentic confession and prayers for forgiveness, a third and equally important aspect of the sense of truth remains. We also must learn again for our time how to speak truthfully our witness to what God has done and is doing in real life. This is what the African American Christian traditions call *testifying.* It is an act in which persons, often beginning with lamentation or confession, tell of the mercy and grace of God. When practiced with integrity, one person's testimony is received and owned by the whole assembly. This is itself a liturgy of confessing faith. In some communities this is deeply emotional, with shouts of encouragement and affirmation, with communal "Amens" ringing. In other communities it is a quiet, loving, and strong moment.

Most Anglo, mainline, Protestant worship patterns have simply lost this, thinking that it only belongs to Pentecostal or highly evangelical churches. But it should belong to all. One tradition which might help restore the vitality of testimony to mainline Protestants is a service, sadly neglected by all but the Moravians and a few others, known as the Love Feast. In the context of a simple meal, this service includes congregational singing, Scripture reading, and time for testimony. Much of our Sunday morning liturgy could be greatly enhanced if the Love Feast or other form of testimony and prayer could be practiced at other occasions. In cases where people seem too busy to hold such gatherings in homes or on Sunday evenings or weekdays, perhaps the Love Feast could be celebrated on an appropriate Sunday morning, especially as an intergenerational occasion.

Unless we also overcome our reluctance to share our faith experiences honestly—in lament, confession, and testimony—our Sunday gatherings will remain routine. Part of the sense of truth comes when we, out of real-life experience, bear witness to how the God we worship on the Lord's Day is working all day long for good in the world. We can, I think, learn much from these forms of worship which have truth-telling at the center.

Of course, testimony can itself become self-indulgent. We catch ourselves trying to outdo one another with tales of our former squalor and current redemption: "You think you were bad, well. . . . " So faith sharing is not always "Oh what a terrible person I was, but now God has made everything all right." We should be a bit suspicious if we hear this repeated over and over. Not everything need be "all right." We know our own tendencies to elaborate, and to make heroic something we have just begun to experience. But as we mature in worship, developing the balance of Word and sacrament to go with lamentation, confession, and testimony, we will know how to temper the exaggerations.

Worship at Full Stretch

All of this is already implied by the extraordinary passage from Ephesians:

> For this reason I bow my knees before the Father, from whom every family in heaven and on earth takes its name. I pray that, according to the riches of his glory, he may grant that you may be strengthened in your inner being with power through his Spirit, and that Christ may dwell in your hearts through faith, as you are being rooted and grounded in love. I pray that you may have the power to comprehend, with all the saints, what is the breadth and length and height and depth, and to know the love of Christ that surpasses knowledge, so that you may be filled with all the fullness of God. (Ephesians 3:14-19)

Christian liturgy, seen in this light, has nothing to fear about being more truthful. To speak the truth in love requires worship "at full stretch." This is worship that knows both the full range of God's Word and the awe and mystery of God in the sacraments and in one another—worship that takes delight in the goodness of God and God's creation. And now we have added the demands of truthfulness. So we must be about stretching ourselves to bring the ancient and contemporary forms to life, and to bring all our life's experience to the God of truth.

CHAPTER FOUR

The Sense of Hope

◆

Hope of the world, thou Christ of great compassion,
speak to our fearful hearts by conflict rent.
Save us, thy people, from consuming passion,
who by our own false hopes and aims are spent.

—GEORGIA HARKNESS, "HOPE OF THE WORLD"

These lines, written over forty years ago, express a deep yearning of the human heart. They plead what so many feel in our present circumstances. Even those who have never sung this hymn recognize the honesty of such a prayer to Jesus. We all have held many false hopes and illusions. So we wonder: What sense of hope does Christian worship offer?

There is a nervous edge to many of our conversations about American society and the larger world these days. For many, life is marked by fearfulness, and a growing sense of losing control. "It all seems so hopeless," is a phrase I've heard over and over recently. When familiar landmarks disappear and we find older optimism fading on many fronts, we come face to face with real choices. We can retreat to whatever space of security we can manage, shutting off any larger hope, or we must learn again to cry out with the words of the psalmist: "Turn, O LORD! How long? Have compassion on your servants!" (Psalm 90:13). Hope remains a stranger until we learn again that our laments carry hope in the very crying out.

It has been easy to confuse hope with optimism. The politeness and easy optimism that mark those of us who have been relatively comfortable in North American society have pervaded much of our church life. When what we sing and preach and pray substitutes a naive optimism for Christian hope, receptivity to the promises of God is dulled. If our worship succeeds only in comforting and consoling, without arousing our yearning for the reality of the divine promises, then only half a gospel is known. If worship skillfully reinforces our notion that we can improve ourselves and our situation if only we try harder, without addressing our need for grace, then the gospel is subverted.

I confess, dear reader, that I prefer the illusions of easy optimism to the vulnerability and work of Christian hope. Do you struggle with this? Does your congregation? If so, perhaps it is time for all of us to admit together our complicity. We have come to expect so little of our worship and common life with respect to the hope of the whole world, that we make an uneasy separate peace with the issues. I find myself at times admitting that I am afraid to take God's promises for the world seriously, for to do so would change my life too radically. Ironically, many of the times when this point hits home to me are precisely in the context of the liturgy! It is as though, even in the humblest gathering about the Word, the water, and the table of the Lord's meal, God does not want us to forget. God will not let us. Yet we habitually do not prepare to remember the hope.

Life Through Hope and Memory

Remembering the hope by praising, thanking, confessing, and interceding is at the heart of Christian life. It is at the heart of Christian worship. How easy it is to forget to remember God in a culture of self-preoccupation and forgetful distraction. The communal memory, yes, the dangerous and grace-filled memory of the whole story of God and the world is at stake. Without the living remembrance about the font, the book, and the table of Christ, there will be no worship in spirit and in truth. Thus, when the child asks the ritual questions at a Passover Seder, "Why is this night different from all other nights?" the answer is the story recalled and retold. That story, which is part of the meaning of our meal with Jesus in the Eucharist, speaks of deliverance and of the present hope: on this night we are crossing over from death to life, from bondage to freedom. Hope depends upon living memory made palpable.

But what are we to hope for? This is a question asked by many, both within and outside our churches, who have settled uneasily into cynicism or a practical atheism in everyday life. Christian worship is a time and place where this question should be asked. "Why are you cast down, O my soul," asks the psalmist, "and why are you disquieted within me? Hope in God; for I shall again praise him, my help and my God" (Psalm 42:11). This speaks so clearly to the nervous movements of our hearts. At the same time, such words—even if they seem not ours at first—are necessary if we are to find our way back to life with God and with one another. The laments, individual and communal, we touched upon in chapter 3 assume that human hope is ultimately rooted in God alone. This is why, when our lives are filled with fear, regret, bitterness, or disillusionment, the act of crying out to someone is a strange evidence that we hope to be heard.

Moving from Everyday Hopes to Deepest Longings

But the plain fact is that human beings *do* hope, even in the midst of despairing circumstances. How else can we account for the survival of African Americans under the humiliating yoke of slavery? How else can we account for the long history of the hope for Zion? How else can we account for the diary of Anne Frank, or for the survival of so many South Africans under apartheid? Even under such immense pressure against hope, do we not desire to be hopeful, beginning with small, everyday things?

We hope for good weather, we hope our children are kept safe, we hope for a time of rest, or for many simple pleasures. All this is part of the weave of everyday life for most people, whether poor or not. Out of everyday wants and wishes, and weekend hopes, a faint glimmer of linkages with Christian hope may spring. Out of the child's "Now I lay me down to sleep" emerge the conditions for more enduring hopes, for this world and for the next. None of this should be ignored by the church. Ordinary, hard-working people who find little time or encouragement for larger-scale hope bring what they have.

Our very ordinariness as human beings can put us in touch, if we are given the time and place for memory, with something essential to authentic Christian worship and life: the rhythm of promise, expectation, and fulfillment. This is the great rhythm of God's way with us, and of the pattern of God's continuing redemptive work in the world. In discovering the story of those creating and liberating promises, Christian worshipers may be encouraged to make the connections between everyday hopes and the deepest hopes which we have so little language and time to express.

Worship-Shaped Hope

Christian hope is not simply our garden-variety wishes and wants dressed up in religious language. Mere wishful thinking or sentimental moods induced by music and prayer will not do. Neither can Christian hope finally be achieved by the cultivation of our intellect or our moral sense, though these efforts are part of the hoping. No, Christian hope is acquired as a gift in the process of living and worshiping in a community shaped over time by the whole story of God and the world—nature and history, heaven and earth together. This is why searching the Scriptures, participating in the bath and the meal, and attending to works of mercy and justice are conditions under which the gift is given. Along with faith and love, hope is part of the blood stream and the heartbeat of Christian life. This is part of the learning and the struggling to live the way of life witnessed to in the Christian Scriptures. At the same time, hope is necessary for our becoming fully human.

The problem for many, however, is not with the theological claim that hope is necessary and central. The problem is that for many, our public worship of

God seems not to arouse and nourish the kind of hope the gospel proclaims. Let us turn to why this is so. Then we may also discover what we may do to reacquaint ourselves with the practice of hope in our assemblies.

Avoiding the Demands of Hope

Again, the problem for most of us is not with the theological claim that hope is central to faith and is necessary for human life to flourish. The problem is often that our public worship of God seems to be out of touch with the actual practices of hope in everyday life. Our liturgies seem not to engender and nourish the kind of hope which the gospel of Christ proclaims. Why is this so?

Any adequate answer to this question would take us well beyond these few pages. Here we touch upon the same complex of social-cultural and spiritual-moral issues we noted in the previous chapters. But some things are clear. Churches, for the most part, prefer to avoid the most difficult and challenging aspects of faith. I do; and most of the congregations with whom I have ministered would prefer to avoid taking on the demands of hope. This does not deny that we have all kinds of desires for the church to do better, to grow in faith. Nonetheless, I hear myself and others say that the great themes of social hope, of hope for the world, are simply overshadowed by personal needs.

Our liturgies cannot offer a prophetic and enlivening sense of hope for the world when we are preoccupied with our own burdens and personal issues. Yet when we do shift our focus to the needs of the world, we are often simply overwhelmed by the moral pain that keeps coming at us through TV, radio, and the newspapers. It is easier for pastors, musicians, and congregations to settle for the pleasant and the comforting, or perhaps for advice and support for getting through the week. This is never to be despised. But what God offers us in authentic Christian worship can be so much more.

Neglecting Biblical Hope

But if one reason why our worship seems weak in forming us in hope is our wishing to avoid the demands of faith, a second reason is our ignorance of Scripture and the larger tradition of Christian moral life. If our hymns and sermons and prayers are always about hope *beyond* this world, it will be difficult to grasp the gift of Christian hope *for* the world. If, on the other hand, all we hope for is becoming more well-adjusted in our life on earth and we are never taken in worship to the "threshold of heaven," we are still impoverished.

Certainly one of the great contributions to a renewed sense of the Bible's social vision has come from twentieth-century liberation theologies of various kinds—from African, African American, Latin American, and feminist Christian sources. For all their differences, liberation theologies have focused on the social and political transformative power of God. Impatient with how the Bible has been used to justify an oppressive status quo, these practical theologies highlight the prophetic promises of God in Jesus Christ. Of equal importance has been the recovery of the great themes of the sacraments, especially baptism and Eucharist. I have been greatly impressed by the combination of deeper biblical study and renewed emphasis on sacramental celebration and participation in the past two decades. But many congregations are still starved for such teaching and such experienced deepening of sacramental life. Ignorance of God's covenantal promises, the prophetic social vision which flows from them, and the very meaning of the water bath and the meal of hope, is widespread. Yet the desire of most congregations to study and to participate more fully in Word and sacrament is great. Could it be that the place to begin renewing worship as the congregation's corporate act of hope is with focused biblical and sacramental learning?

The Character and Quality of Our Corporate Worship

There is yet a third, more obvious reason for our worship's failure to build us up in hope: the character and quality of how we actually worship together. This includes the style of leadership, the involvement of the laity, the forms of prayer, the manner of baptism and renewal, and the way we practice Holy Communion. Many persons whom I have interviewed about their worship experience consistently name three factors that prevent their deeper participation: (1) when worship is "done *for* us"; (2) when worship is "done *to* us"; and (3) when "we don't understand what is going on." Each of these factors bears directly upon the style and substance of Christian liturgy.

The first is, unfortunately, too common. When the preacher and the singers do everything, and there is no active engagement on the part of the remaining congregation, hope remains at best only talked or sung about. This is not simply found in small rural churches where, as we often hear, the "people don't want to do anything but listen and sing a hymn or two." This is not fair to the experience of many smaller churches. To do worship for the congregation is a temptation for larger churches with paid professional staff. In this case, the laity may be used to having the "professionals" do it. As I heard a prominent banker say to the musician, "We pay you to be the experts, so do worship well."

The second factor that prevents worship from becoming a corporate act of hope is when effort is expended largely on entertaining or dramatically manipulating the congregation. All authentic worship has a dramatic element. One cannot read the Bible over time, or enact the feast of Christmas, Easter, or Pentecost without being taken into the dramatic narrative of Jesus Christ. But when the aim is concentrated solely on eliciting a response from the pews, something intrinsic to worship is lost. Liturgy is the corporate act of the people of God, who bring life to the forms of preaching, song, and prayer. We struggle to provide patterns and forms of speaking and acting by which the congregation may receive and respond to the mystery of God in Christ. When worship is viewed and practiced primarily as a means to an end—whether conversion or aesthetic enjoyment—it loses its character as the hope-filled offering of praise and thanksgiving to God.

The third factor inhibiting the development of authentic Christian hope is lack of education. In a recent study of thirteen United Methodist congregations, I found that very few had offered regular, sustained study of the hymnal, either for the learning of new hymns and psalms, or for the formation of the congregation in understanding the basic elements in the principal services. Some are providing increasingly helpful information in one area or another, but few have yet begun the more comprehensive task of introducing the congregation over time to the whole "canon" of Christian worship: Christian initiation (baptism and baptismal renewal), the Lord's Supper (Eucharist), daily prayer, the cycles of the Christian calendar, and various "rites of passage" (funerals, marriages, healing services, reconciliation services, rites of blessing and leave-taking, as well as others). But where such teaching, sometimes known by the ancient word "catechesis," is a priority, the quality and level of participation increases remarkably. To undertake these changes, both in our style of celebrating the gospel, and in our method of congregational education, is already an act of hope. This is the upbuilding of the church in love of which Paul speaks in his letters to the churches.

The Practice of Hope

When we avoid the demands of hope, when we neglect our biblical heritage of hope, when the very character and quality of our worship stifles hope, we miss God's grace at the heart of the church's mission. Fortunately, recognizing the problems helps us move toward solutions. There are many things we can do that will help us rediscover the practice of hope in our assemblies.

Not long ago, I spoke with a family who told me about the congregations they had belonged to over the last fifteen years. The first was a small-town church much like the one in which their parents had grown up. It was, as they described it, a comfortable place where people knew one another. The Sunday gathering was friendly and unpretentious. There was much they liked about being there, especially as a family with two young children. But a conflict arose between the pastor and one of the leading families over whether to allow a divorced persons' support group to meet. Everyone knew about the dispute, and talked a great deal about it outside the church. Finally, the family asked the pastor to allow the whole congregation to pray together about the matter. For a long time he hesitated, for fear of what those who opposed the idea might do: "I wish it were possible, but everyone's too stubborn." The mother replied, "Let's stop wishing and start waiting in prayer."

On a Sunday some weeks later, a person in the prayer group was appointed to lead the Sunday morning prayer. Very gently, she included among the prayers that morning a request that the congregation be given patience and courage to discern God's will for broken families. On Monday, a member of the "ruling family" called the pastor to say they had changed their mind about the divorce support group, admitting that one of their own family had been holding on to an abusive marriage. Maybe the church could help someone like her. It was that period of active waiting and shared public prayer that made Christian hope real for them all.

Henri Nouwen has observed, "Hope is trusting that something will be fulfilled, but fulfilled according to the promises and not just according to our wishes."[1] Waiting in hope is active. It is close to the Quaker practice of "holding someone in the Light." This is a radical attitude because it does mean giving over our control—or our fear that something will not be possible—to God. This I find to be rare among the whole congregation in most of our churches. Smaller groups are more likely to be the places where such practices begin, though even there our control needs or our fears may prevent active waiting from touching the larger community.

A congregation in another city recently began holding a healing service once a month. A single woman in her late twenties, having just moved to that city, began visiting there and learned of the monthly Wednesday evening service. She admitted that her image of healing was that of the dramatic TV healers. But a friend persuaded her to attend. As others, after receiving Communion, made their way to places of anointing and prayer—older and younger, married and single, of different racial backgrounds—she suddenly realized "how absolutely safe" she felt here. The simple, honest approach to the offer of healing for body, memory, relationships, and inner turmoil was a profound act of hope. She said, "I finally sensed why Jesus asked, 'Which is it easier to say, "rise, take up your bed and walk," or "your sins are forgiven"?' " That congregation practices what the gospel offers: physical and spiritual healing are both part of the grace of Christ; but both require worshipful sensitivity and honest, patient, active waiting. "The Lord's Supper itself," she said, "has taken on the meaning of healing to me now. I never knew that before." We have somewhere to take the pain and the hope.

A Common Journey of Hope

We are invited to give an account of the hope within us—to live hopefully as well as to speak hope to the world. This, I am convinced, requires a fresh look at the relationship between liturgy and our common life. At the root of so much of our so-called "problem with worship," and the various debates currently raging between "traditional" and "contemporary" styles, is the lack of sustained common life. We should rightly hope for changed lives, for spiritual encouragement, and for ministries that make a difference in our local communities and the larger world. Christian worship bears, at its heart, the promises of God to sustain us in hope. This is not something done for us or to us by worship leaders. Rather it is the mystery of grace into which we journey together. Worship is the continuing rehearsal of God's hope for us.

The Longing Not to Be Forgotten

Perhaps more than we hope for changed lives and circumstances, even more than we hope for specific physical healings, I sense that most of us hope that we will not be forgotten or abandoned—that we will be remembered. The deepest hope in times of chaos and change is that God will not forget us. This was ancient

Israel's hope, and it is still ours today. The awareness of such a hope is found in our remembering of God and God's remembering of the covenant people—this is the central story of how worship is related to salvation. Forgetting God is not mere laziness or even emotional dullness, it is an act of worshiping false hopes—our idols. To forget God's Word and offer of grace is to break the promise, by forgetting the orphans, the widows, the oppressed. Neglecting justice and kindness—failing to walk humbly with God in care for one another—is itself a forgetting of God. But these are precisely what authentic worship is set against!

Christian worship, over time, with all its variety of forms and patterns, contains the promise of God not to forget: to bless and to sustain, to heal and to reconcile. This is what John's Gospel intends when it speaks of "eternal life." It begins here and now. Life in the community of Jesus Christ is to be a participation in that quality of life already, even though the character of eternal life is not yet apparent in its fullness. Life is a gift received and lived in gratitude and hope. We may miss this sense because our worship life is not grounded deeply in our common ministries and learning. This is why we must recover the concrete ways in which we can weep with those who suffer and cry out, laugh with those who rejoice, and be honored when others are honored.

Shared Ministry Produces Hope

The sense of hope lies yet ahead for us. When liturgy is reconnected to common ministry and learning, hope will spring forth, like the flowers blossoming in the desert Isaiah envisioned. In several congregations I know, a common commitment to building houses for Habitat for Humanity has fostered precisely such a blossoming of hope. After searching for various solutions to the problem of "routine" worship, they discovered that, for them, the solution was not first in the sanctuary at all. It involved finding a connection between what was done outside and inside the sanctuary. As one person put it, "Our being able to build that house together was one of the most revolutionary things to happen in a long time." Another added, "We got outside of ourselves and plugged into others' real life. We finally had something to pray about besides ourselves, and when we finished, we had something to praise God for."

Many ministries go on quietly and undramatically in our midst as well. Yet we often overlook the communal prayer rooted in these ministries: "meals on wheels" programs; hospital calling by the laity; various ministries to the sick and bereaved; ministries to new mothers, fathers, and babies; or the commissioning of specific tasks and missions. Specific mention of particular ministries (if it is not merely disguised propaganda or self-congratulation) make visible and palpable the lifeblood of the congregation outside the walls of formal liturgy. We may recall Justin Martyr's description of Sunday morning in a church in Rome in the mid-second century:

> The elements which have been "eucharistized" are distributed and received by each one; and they are sent to the absent by the deacons. Those who are prosperous, if they wish, contribute what each one deems

appropriate; and the collection is deposited with the president [presider]; and he [along with the deacons] takes care of the orphans and widows, and those who are needy because of sickness or other cause, and the captives, and the strangers who sojourn amongst us.[2]

In this very early account of Sunday worship we see the intimate connection between praying, celebrating the Eucharist, and serving others. This is the clue for us today. And yet it is not a special technique. We need not search for some newly devised style in order to emphasize this connection during our Eucharist service—it is given in the Eucharistic action itself, if we have but eyes to behold, ears to hear, and prepared hearts schooled in Jesus' ministry. What may be required is variation in the way Communion is received, or perhaps the introduction of singing during the Communion itself.

In the New Testament churches we note diversity of ministries and gifts of the whole community. We learn of the early community's struggle to order its gifts and ministries as it grew and spread. Paul's marvelous image of the body with many members, each needing the other (Romans 12:4-5), needs to resurface in our worship. Let there be readers, servers, singers, and leaders of prayer springing from actual ministries—let these be hope made audible and visible. The community gathered and the community in service to neighbors near and far are but two sides of the same mystery of common life in Christ. This is exactly what baptism and Eucharist point toward. Liturgy is not "playing church," but the formation and expression of God's grace in human form. Hope is always tempered with courage and realism, and thus kept from being mere optimism, wishful thinking, or utopian dreaming.

Learning Attentiveness

There are things we can do together to restore a sense of hope to our common worship. These I have just mentioned show us that much depends upon what goes on outside our rooms and immediate environments for liturgy. The real starting point may also be located in developing anew (or for the first time) the practice of listening well to one another.

To practice attending to the hopes and fears that govern our lives is essential. This is not to be confined to the pastor's one-on-one counseling sessions, though God knows we need it there. I speak of setting out to recover levels of spiritual attentiveness and discernment with one another in nonthreatening ways, and in many places and groups. Part of John Wesley's genius was his creation of such forums for listening in the class meetings and societies of his ministry. Hope springs forth as a noticeable quality of gathered worship when a congregation begins to listen honestly and attentively to one another. This is not a coercive or compulsive act, as in some "hothouse" of spirituality. Rather, the qualities of genuine respect and care and a sense of the mystery of life should pervade our worshiping assembly. Again, this allows us to experience in our worship the act of weeping and rejoicing with one another. Our singing, our praying, our listening to the Word in Scripture and sermon, and our common meal together thus become the means of grace and a mutual sign of hope.

Perhaps at the root of our hesitancy is also a basic fear. Perhaps after all is said and done, we may fear the promises of God. We may be like the Israelites whose eyes were shut and ears stopped, lest they "turn and be healed" (Isaiah 6:10). For such promises and such a love will indeed reveal our false hopes and illusions. Such making of connections between God's love made visible and audible in common ministries and in the Word and sacrament in all occasions for worship is that radical. In the whole range of Christian liturgy—informal and formal, Word and sacrament, familiar and challenging—we are offered bread from heaven. But too often, we miss it because we are distracted. Like the cats in our household when someone points to the food in their bowls, we may simply stare at the end of the finger that points. We must learn again to look in the direction Christ's love points. Then we can experience anew the true hope of the world.

Of the many biblical passages which express the centrality of hope, two deserve final mention in this chapter. The first is the admonition that we are to give an "accounting for the hope that is in [us]" (1 Peter 3:15). Can we see now that every gathering is such an account? Every act of song and prayer and common meal is an act of hope in this world, provided that it looks in the direction God's love looks. At the heart of our common baptism, in all our passages through time, this hope is offered again and again to our human senses.

The second passage is in that inexhaustible twelfth chapter of Paul's letter to Rome: we are to "rejoice in [our] hope" (Romans 12:12). This is the overflowing sign of hope, that it leads to a common joy, whether solemn or ecstatic, quiet or boisterous. But we need to realize that this joy is more than immediate good feeling, though it certainly brings such moments of experience. This is a rejoicing in the divine hope, a way to live hopefully. Why else would Walt McFarland, a member of an inner-city church I once served, after the arduous journey of attending to his wife's long terminal illness, say to me, "I can't explain it, but it's been a joy." He was not denying for one instant the frustrations, the bad days of pain, or the weariness he had known. Rather, he was rejoicing in his hope in God. For he knew that the suffering love of Christ had been there in that room, at the bedside with them, even to the end, when blessed rest and release came.

I tell you, such a sense of hope waits for us. It is found in singing James Weldon Johnson's hymn "Lift Every Voice and Sing":

> Sing a song full of the faith that the dark past has taught us;
> sing a song full of the hope that the present has brought us.[3]

The hope is in a hundred hymns, it permeates Scripture, it is enacted when we baptize, it is given in every Holy Communion, it is extended to us in the recovery of healing services, and it is formed in us if we rediscover daily common prayer. But it requires of us the vulnerability of an Advent expectancy. We live east of Eden, and between the times of God's incarnation and the consummation of all things in Christ.

Congregations can begin to rediscover such expectancy by learning to practice the season of Advent more faithfully. By studying the prophetic readings and the gospel texts, and by entering more deeply together into the yearnings of Israel and the cry of the early church, "Come, Lord Jesus," we will understand just how deeply God has entered into human life and history. The tensions of the "already" of Jesus' birth, life, death, and resurrection, and the "not yet" of our world are sung and prayed in these Sundays. Here we are formed in something other than the deceptive commercial promises of a Merry Christmas.

Authentic Christian worship, true to its sources and alert to the present realities of human life, is a school of hope. This is not superficial optimism, for it trains us for the reign of God yet to come. It arouses in us a passion for what the prophets spoke of: a time of justice and peace, a time of human reconciliation with God, a time of abundance and the healing of the nations.

Our true hope lies in once again learning to join the prophetic-priestly Jesus in ongoing prayer and action in the world. Such liturgy is both praise *and* service. If Christ is the hope of the world, then we do well to bring our hopes and fears to the place he promised to meet us—where two or three gather in his name about the book, the font, and the table. We can there learn again, for our time and place, how to join his continual intercession for the whole world.

Afterword

O taste and see that the LORD is good.
—PSALM 34:8

The Christian assembly for worship is a gathering for hearing, speaking, singing, seeing, washing, drinking, feeding and being fed, greeting, and dancing. Sometimes we do all these things, as in the great Easter Vigil; sometimes we do only a few, as in daily prayer. In all such gatherings, large or small, God is encountered through the senses. We cannot avoid the human means by which grace is offered and received, whether in the full enthusiasm of a Pentecostal prayer meeting, or in the restraint of Anglican compline. Part of the mystery of how we come to know and to be known in the divine life resides here. What the psalmist sings is true: "O taste and see that the LORD is good."

Yet worship is not simply a matter of the physical senses. If that were all, we could expect to make liturgy "work" by stimulating the greatest range of bodily sensation. The most effective participation of people in public worship would then be achieved by finding the best way to activate our immediate feeling states. This is a tempting strategy, and one that is especially available through electronic means and controlled staging.

Rock concerts are unmistakably ritual events for many. I have been impressed with their sheer physicality. The level of amplification, the screaming of the fans, and the dancing are totally engaging. Yet if one asks about what is sung, when words are employed, it is the wrong question. In most cases the kinetic and aural response of the hearers is not directly related to what is sung, but to the intensity and physical reaction of the body to the level of sound, and to the rhythmic component. The mind and the heart are not equally engaged.

Because God is remembered and addressed, and truthfulness is a necessary quality in an event of worship, something more than bodily participation is at stake. In these pages I have been exploring worship that engages the "senses"—both the physical senses and the senses of the mind and heart, which is to say the soul. By this I refer to what the Scripture means in commanding that we love God with all our heart and mind and strength (Deuteronomy 6:5, Matthew 22:35, Mark 12:30). Miriam and Moses sing to the Lord, not simply about themselves. David dances before the ark of the covenant. Ambiguous though this may be, it shows ecstatic joy in God's presence, not merely self-expression. When the two disciples share a meal with a strange companion one evening at Emmaus, they receive more than the taste of bread and wine. So the church at prayer and song enacts and receives more than its own cultural expression.

In the worshiping assembly, we remember with our bodily participation the promises, and invoke the presence remembered in Word, bath, and holy meal. Here we bring our sense of being alive in the world, our sense of restlessness, our sense of sorrow, our sense of gratitude, our hopes and fears, and all our questions. What emerges in living ritual action is a vision of the world as the arena of God's creative and redemptive glory. It is also the arena of God's will which we come slowly to pray for and occasionally to realize.

This is why worship is so central to the Christian life. Without the assembly to continually remember, proclaim, and faithfully enact the story of God in the world and in our lives, we could not form, much less give expression to, the sense of God. John Wesley, drawing upon earlier Eastern Christianity and a longer tradition of the idea of "spiritual senses," proposed that God provides us with ways to sense God.

Our journey here offers a reminder that, without a sense of awe, of delight, of truthfulness, and of hope, our liturgies lack something essential—essential to who God is, and essential to who we are invited by grace to become. These "senses," along with others yet to be explored, are ways in which we come to know God.

Knowing God Means Sharing God's Passion

Knowing God is more than knowing about God, more than simply affirming right belief. Knowing God is more than simply "experiencing" God inwardly. Rather, to know God is to love, adore, fear, rejoice in, and hope in God over time and in all circumstances. Such love and hope, if grounded in the truth, can never be presumptuous or a matter of prideful possession. We cannot possess God. If we think we do, faith diminishes, and common life loses its vibrancy. Therefore, reverence and awe in the presence of God are necessary.

To come into the presence of God brings "fear and trembling," not of God's wrathful judgment, but of God's holy compassion for us and for the world. Such fear is not the same as terror in front of an enemy. It is a sense of the enormous suffering love of God for the creation and for all things, great and small within it, including us. Only with such a sense of holiness will we also begin to see these very creatures, "great and small," as "bright and beautiful," as the children's hymn sings. Worship is a time and place where we find our best being in the movement from awe to delight, from honesty before God to hope. By loving deeply and delighting in what God has made, we can begin to receive the mystery of our own lives back. Fred Pratt Green has put this well in his hymn "When in Our Music God Is Glorified":

> When in our music God is glorified,
> and adoration leaves no room from pride,
> it is as though the whole creation cried
> Alleluia![1]

To delight in and care for the very being of that which God loves so much—that is itself awesome. To sing "Alleluia" with all creation restored is true worship.

Learning the Heights and Depths

I must be continually reminded, and hence remind churches that our liturgies cannot long be faithful without attention to the senses. Remarkably, we are not left to our own devices, or bid simply to find out what the surrounding culture, popular or highly trained, provides. We keep on rediscovering the interrelated senses of awe, delight, truthfulness, and hope. These are not sequenced steps we can neatly program for better worship. They are features of what we experience when God becomes real. Just as a nourishing diet requires all the basic food groups, Christian worship in the common assembly requires all of these senses. One-sided, easy praise, without a sense of solidarity in the world's suffering, will threaten to keep us from understanding the depth and the mystery of God's entering into our suffering world. But unrelieved lamentation and oppressive naming of sin that never turns in trust and hope to God's promises contradicts God's offer of grace in Christ. Christian worship, like a dazzling diamond, must continually be turned in the light of our living and dying, our struggles and our deepest hopes, in order to be fully appreciated. Like a diamond, worship can, through the feasts and seasons of God's grace, reveal its many facets.

Each community of worship must ask, how do we experience and practice these four senses? Despite our various differences in theological accent—whether we lean to more or less informality or spontaneity in worship—these senses are basic to the worship of God.

I consider it wonderfully hopeful that the whole pattern of these senses of God's gracious self-giving may be revealed through any one of the particular senses; just as the mystery of true encounter with God found in the whole liturgy may be revealed in one small element in the service. A hymn, a single image or phrase, a psalm, something in a prayer, the sermon, a touch from a neighbor in our sorrow, a gesture of welcome to the table, the trembling hand stretched to receive the bread or cup, or the testimony of a friend—these lie in wait at any time to evoke in us the sense of God.

Any of us who have sung "For All the Saints" at the funeral of a beloved, will find, from time to time, in the singing of that hymn, a return of the grief mingled with joy. And so we need not be embarrassed when our voice cracks, or we simply must stop singing and be carried by the song of the congregation surrounding us—this is the wonder and the awe of Christian worship. It is never predictable, much less a matter of manipulation. Yet we can attend to the conditions under which a community may grow into such a larger mystery of God with us.

From Cultural Ferment to Discernment

It is easy to be critical of various "cultural captivities" which may prevent our worship from shaping our daily lives more directly. It is easy to speak of crisis, or of failure to achieve results, or of the lack of certain experiences. But in the end, none of these captivities can separate us from God's grace. In appealing for a recovery of a deeper sense of awe or delight or truthfulness or hope, I have in mind real pastoral situations where we can, together, search out the means of grace.

The current debates over the cultural relevance and the evangelical appeal of our worship are important. The church has nothing to gain in smothering debate or ignoring ethnic, gender, or cultural differences. This is as true of debate over worship in contemporary

North American culture as it was, and is, of debate over true and false prophecy. We are in a period of many voices calling for many different strategies. But we are also now in a place where ferment can lead to discernment.

From my own considerable involvement in "experimental worship" in the sixties, I realize now that our current situation is not unique. Many current proposals for "contemporary worship" have a history running back through earlier times of seeking new relevance. These harken back to the American frontier and to the permanent tension between "relevance" and "identity" within Christian faith and life. Our current problem lies not with the "irrelevance" of much of the larger Christian tradition that we may discard or overlook, but with the lack of connection between the gathered community's worship of God and our actual suffering and rejoicing, our hopes and fears, and the restlessness of true joy.

* * * * *

We began with a big question: What makes Christian worship true and relevant, and how can our liturgical gatherings shape and express authentic Christian faith and life in the world of everyday? I have tried to answer this by exploring the four senses which seem essential to Christian worship. Along the way, we have noted specific ways in which to set the conditions for nurturing our common life in these senses. When relevance is stressed as a strategy for creating "experiences," we may lose what is most fundamental to the worship of God in Christ Jesus. There is, I believe, an abiding restlessness in every community of faith— given all our cultural and social diversities—for both relevance and identity in God. There is, therefore, a relevance in growing together into Christ. We always must begin where we are, with what we have inherited. Once we have named and acknowledged our position, then opens the possibility of asking about the way we gather about the Word, the font, and the table of the Lord.

What is at stake, finally, are the very means of grace we have received from Christ, attested to in Scripture and the living traditions of authentic Christianity. To these we must always return in every historical period of change, and in each distinctive church's ongoing life. Where our actual practices or our neglect of the essentials make us culturally captive—as the current "culture of immediacy" has—then we must set out to listen, to pray, and to exercise the means of grace with awe, delight, truthfulness, and hope. All these, our restless hearts will discover, are grounded in the incarnate, Spirit-breathing life of God for the sake of the world.

NOTES

Chapter 1. The Sense of Awe

1. Abraham Heschel, *God in Search of Man* (New York: Meridian Books, 1959), 251.

2. Jaroslav Vajda, "God of the Sparrow God of the Whale," in *The United Methodist Hymnal* (Nashville: The United Methodist Publishing House, 1989), no. 122.

3. Gerard Manley Hopkins, "Hurrahing in Harvest," in *Poems of Gerard Manley Hopkins,* third edition, ed. Helen Gardner (New York and London: Oxford University Press, 1948), 75.

Chapter 2. The Sense of Delight

1. Isaac Watts, "Praise Ye the Lord," a version of Psalm 147, cited in *Duty and Delight: Routley Remembered,* ed. Robin A. Leaver, James H. Litton, and Carlton R. Young (Carol Stream, Ill.: Hope Publishing Company, 1985), xiii.

2. Erik Routley, "For Musicians," written in 1976, cited in *Duty and Delight: Routley Remembered,* xiii.

3. C. S. Lewis, *Reflections on the Psalms* (New York: Harcourt, Brace and World, 1958), 95.

4. Traditional text of "My Dancing Day" is found in *The Oxford Book of Carols,* ed. Percy Dearmer, R. Vaughan Williams, and Martin Shaw (London: Oxford University Press, 1928), 158-59.

5. Sydney Carter, "Lord of the Dance," in *Songs of Sydney Carter: in the Present Tense* (Norfolk, England: Galliard, 1963), 4-5.

6. Romano Guardini, in *The Spirit of the Liturgy* (New York: Benziger, 1931), speaks of Christian liturgy as both serious and playful. This quality requires form and freedom to improvise, and is much like playing the blues or jazz, or making surprising discoveries in children's games.

Chapter 3. The Sense of Truth

1. Howard A. Walter, "I Would Be True," in *The Book of Hymns* (Nashville: United Methodist Publishing House, 1964), no. 156.

2. Gail Ramshaw, *Words That Sing* (Chicago: Liturgy Training Publications, 1992), 28.

3. Ibid.

4. Brian Wren, "When Pain and Terror Strike by Chance," in *New Beginnings: 30 New Hymns for the 90s* (Carol Stream, Ill.: Hope Publishing Company, 1993), no. 11.

5. Brian Wren, "God, Give Us Freedom to Lament," in *New Beginnings*, no. 26.

6. C. S. Lewis, *Letters to Malcolm: Chiefly on Prayer* (New York: Harcourt, Brace and World, 1963), 82.

7. Collect for Purity, the Opening Prayer from A Service of Word and Table I, *The United Methodist Hymnal* (Nashville: The United Methodist Publishing House, 1989), 6.

Chapter 4. The Sense of Hope

1. Henri J. M. Nouwen, "A Spirituality of Waiting," *Weavings* 2, no. 1 (January-February 1987): 10.

2. Justin Martyr, "The First Apology of Justin Martyr," trans. Bard Thompson, in *Liturgies of the Western Church*, ed. Bard Thompson (New York: Word Publishing, 1961), 9.

3. James Weldon Johnson, "Lift Every Voice and Sing," in *The United Methodist Hymnal* (Nashville: The United Methodist Publishing House, 1989), no. 519.